# Anxiety

The Comprehensive Beginner's Guide To Rewire & Retrain Your Anxious Brain & Stop Panic Attacks

*(Defeat And Recovery From Depression)*

**Panteleimon Kostopoulos**

# TABLE OF CONTENT

Chapter 1: Medications That Can Preserve The Health Of The Brain .......... 1

Chapter 3: Keep Learning ......... 19

Chapter 4: Depression's Nine Manifestations. 31

Chapter 5: When Day-To-Day Difficulties Become Overwhelming ............ 38

Chapter 6: What It Takes to Maintain Weight Loss: A Gut-Health-Focused Approach .......... 42

Chapter 7: Making the Choice for Recovery — The Path to Healing .......... 60

Chapter 8: Preserving and Improving Your Mental Health .......... 64

Chapter 9: Simple Methods To Fight Stress And Anxiety .......... 71

Chapter 10: Enhancing Productivity And Maintaining A Healthy Work-Life Balance Through Emotional Mastery At Work .......... 83

Chapter 11: Differences Between Bipolar Disorder And Anxiety Disorders ............................ 87

Chapter 12: Key Strategies To De-Stress The Mind ................................................................. 104

Chapter 13: Anxiety Disorders ............................ 116

Chapter 14: Types Of Assistance To Consider ........................................................................... 126

# Chapter 1: Medications That Can Preserve The Health Of The Brain

The brain is the most complex organ in the human body, and maintaining its health is essential for maintaining mental and physical health. There are numerous medications that can be used to maintain brain health.

including medications used to treat depression, anxiety, insomnia, and Alzheimer's.

Antidepressants are a medication used to treat depression, which can be caused by a variety of factors including stress, trauma, and a chemical imbalance in the brain. Selective serotonin reuptake inhibitors (SSRIs) and serotonin-norepinephrine reuptake inhibitors are common antidepressants (SNRIs). These medications can alleviate depressive symptoms such as low mood, loss of interest in activities, and concentration difficulties.

Anxiety medications can also be used to alleviate anxiety symptoms such as excessive worry, restlessness, and difficulty sleeping. Antidepressants and benzodiazepines (Xanax, Valium, and Ativan) are commonly prescribed for anxiety. These medications can help alleviate the severity of anxiety symptoms and improve a person's stress management.

Insomnia is a sleep disorder that causes difficulty falling asleep or staying asleep, and its causes include stress, medications, and certain medical conditions. Medication such as benzodiazepines, non-benzodiazepines (Ambien, Lunesta), and melatonin can reduce insomnia symptoms and improve sleep quality.

Alzheimer's disease is a progressive neurological disorder that results in memory loss, confusion, and difficulty performing daily tasks. Cholinesterase inhibitors (Aricept, Exelon, Razadyne) can slow the disease's progression and improve cognitive function.

Stimulants and nootropics, which are used to improve focus, concentration, and memory, are two additional medications that can help maintain brain health.

memory. Stimulants like Adderall and Ritalin can increase alertness and enhance cognitive performance. Nootropics such as Piracetam and Aniracetam can also aid in memory and concentration enhancement.

In addition to medications, changes in lifestyle, such as regular exercise, a healthy diet, and stress reduction, can aid in maintaining brain health. Regular physical activity increases brain blood flow, which reduces stress and improves cognitive function. A healthy diet that is abundant in fruits and vegetables can provide the brain with vital vitamins and minerals. Reducing stress can also improve mental health and reduce the likelihood of developing depression and anxiety.

In general, medication can be an effective method for maintaining brain health.

However, it is essential to consult your physician before taking any medications and to carefully adhere to their instructions. Additionally, alterations to one's lifestyle, such as regular exercise, a healthy diet, and stress reduction, can promote mental health.

## Chapter 2: The Amygdale and Its Influence on Anxiety

The amygdale are a pair of tiny, almond-shaped nucleus clusters located near the base of your brain.

The amygdala is responsible for assessing the emotional significance of events that occur in your environment by determining whether or not they pose a threat to you.

The amygdala will initiate your body's fight-or-flight response to help you react to a perceived threat if it determines that a vehicle driving towards you on the street is at risk of hitting you or that a rattlesnake is curled up on the rock by your front door.

The flight or fight response, a beneficial aspect of our nature, is designed to protect us by preparing us to escape dangerous situations safely.

However, the fight-or-flight response will develop into chronic worry and anxiety disorders if it is activated when there is no danger or if it is activated too quickly when there is no danger.

In other words, there are both appropriate and inappropriate responses, such as flight and fight.

Your own thoughts, memories, and emotions are common sources of unwarranted flight or fight responses. Anxiety and the fight-or-flight response can be triggered by a fear of one's own thoughts.

The Reaction Chain of Anxiety

The amygdala initiates the mechanisms that produce anxiety and fear in the brain. It is known that animals lacking an amygdala display no signs of fear. For instance, rats lacking an amygdala cuddled up close to cats, one of their natural predators, without fear.

Here is how the amygdala produces fear. When it detects danger, the amygdala transmits nerve signals to the hypothalamus, another region of the brain. After stimulating the adrenal gland, the pituitary gland stimulates the brain. The adrenal gland secretes the chemicals adrenaline, noradrenaline, and cortisol that cause true fear and the fight-or-flight response.

Concern and Anxiety

Consider the difference between fear and anxiety when attempting to differentiate between a normal and adaptable flight or fight response and a maladaptive flight or fight response that causes chronic distress.

Fear is the immediate response to a real threat in your environment. When there is no immediate danger, anxiety is the persistent feeling of being in danger. When anxiety persists in the absence of a threat, it is a symptom of an anxiety disorder.

Unquestionably, the amygdala contributes to the development of fear and persistent anxiety, but it appears that another brain region, the Bed Nucleus of the Stria Terminalis (BSNT), is essential for the transformation of acute fear into chronic anxiety. The

BSNTs of individuals with anxiety disorders are overactive.

The most important takeaway from this situation is that if you experience fear when there is nothing to fear, you may have an anxiety disorder. It would be prudent to consult a physician to determine if you do.

Can Treating Anxiety Aid Our Understanding of the Amygdala?

At the moment, practising mindfulness, meditation, or cognitive behavioural therapy are the greatest approaches to combat anxiety (CBT) (CBT).

However, a recent intriguing study suggests that biofeedback technology may soon make it possible to train the amygdala to respond more strongly to pleasant memories and less strongly to unpleasant ones. This therapy method utilises either EEG or fMRI technology to determine the amygdala's level of activity. You may then use this to learn how to alter the amount that your amygdala is active.

Despite the fact that these technologies are still in development, there is a great deal of optimism that they will soon be available to the general public.

The use of training strategies that shut down the fear response is another potential anxiety therapy that is still in the research stage and has been shown to lessen anxiety. A person's fear response must be extinguished by exposing them to the feared object or situation in a completely safe environment. If a person realises that a feared object, such as a spider or a gun, is not inherently dangerous, their amygdala will no longer trigger a fight or flight response, according to the theory.

Simple Steps to Reduce Present-Moment Anxiety

Here are some simple steps you can take right now to attempt to reduce your anxiety.

• Slow Your Breathing Down and Deepen It: As I scaled a Himalayan cliff face to cross a high pass, I can recall a time when I employed slow, deep breathing to reduce my anxiety. There was a thunderstorm, and I could hear the approaching lightning crackling. I was hyperventilating and gasping for air because I was so terrified and on my face. I took control of my breathing and regained composure. I regulated my breathing and took deep breaths to survive the storm.

There are numerous alternatives to fear exposure that aid the amygdala in maintaining composure. These involve reducing the physical and emotional stresses under your control that influence how strongly you react to external stressors. You may improve your physical and mental health and reduce the likelihood that stressful situations will trigger the amygdala's flight-or-fight response by adhering to the below recommendations.

• Get Organized: Chaos and disorganisation in life can lead to a variety of stresses, such as being late for work or appointments, being unable to find essential items when you need them, receiving feedback from others about your disorganisation, or simply feeling guilty about not being organised. You will feel more confident and in control of your life if you take the time to organise and store items in a location where you (and others) can find them when needed.

• Establish Routines: Routines may be essential for individuals with anxiety. It is reassuring to be able to rely on a few constants, such as eating meals at specific times, going for daily walks, or reading every night before going to bed in the midst of an uncertain day. The consistency of routines may reassure you that you have the freedom to live your life as you wish and help to alleviate any apprehensive feelings caused by unexpected events.

• Schedule Free Time: Many people believe they cannot afford free time, despite the fact that it is a valuable and necessary resource. When you have work to complete, bills to pay, and errands to run from the moment you wake up until the moment you fall asleep, it may be difficult to imagine finding any time for yourself. It is essential to keep in mind that free time is valuable enough to schedule. Free time allows you to check in with yourself and assess how you feel about various aspects of your life, which is particularly beneficial if you suffer from anxiety. Rather than letting troubling issues fester in the back of your mind and develop into obsessive thought patterns, you may choose to focus your energy on resolving them.

• Practice meditation (or join a group): During meditation, you can reflect on your life, just as you can during free time. Additionally, it offers you the ability to temporarily set aside your issues and concentrate on "being." This may seem like ignoring your issues, but that is not what meditation is about. Meditation is all about developing disciplined thinking, which can help you break free from the depressing thought patterns linked to your triggers, which kick off panic episodes in the amygdala.

• Get Adequate Rest: If you want to maintain a healthy body and mind, you must get a good night's sleep every night (eight to nine hours for most people). Set a bedtime and adhere to it to train your mind to go to sleep at a certain time. To promote REM sleep, you should also sleep in complete darkness (or with a sleep mask) and avoid caffeine for at least four hours before bedtime. In addition to allowing your mind a well-deserved vacation, sufficient REM sleep allows your body to recover overnight.

• Eat Well: When anxiety depletes your body's resources, you must replenish them by eating a healthy, balanced diet. When combined with the right type of physical activity, such as 30 minutes of steady exercise three times per week, it is an excellent way to keep your body feeling fit and healthy, which may influence your perception of your ability to handle obstacles. In addition, it may assist with heart rate regulation, preventing excessive heart rates caused by anxiety from jeopardising your health or even your life.

When you notice that the almond-shaped portion of your brain is functioning excessively, but you cannot see or feel it, there are several things you can do to maintain control. Taking care of your body and mind should be your top priority. Once you've accomplished this, you'll be better equipped to deal with life's stresses, and you may be able to retrain your amygdala to stop overreacting to things that don't actually pose a threat but make you anxious nonetheless.

## Chapter 3: Keep Learning

The capacity and willingness to learn are valuable skills that can be advantageous in many aspects of your life, including your career. Learning can occur in the traditional sense through reading and studying, or in a more interpersonal sense through listening. It is an essential component of personal development in any case.

Education has always had a financial impact. For many people, education may feel like a luxury. On the other hand, individuals seeking to expand their knowledge have more resources than ever before. There are numerous study options, including the use of free online programmes and library resources.

Intelligent coaches attempt to market their expertise for the benefit of others by developing low-cost courses, but we are so obsessed with free stuff.

We are not interested in purchasing courses, investing in our education, studying, or exerting significant effort to gain.

However, this will not be the case because we all have different destinies and paths to follow. Remember that what works for Mr. A may not work for Mr. B but will work for Mr. C; such is life; we just need to view it from different angles.

You do not need to attend college to acquire these skills; they are occupational skills, and you can obtain them by purchasing courses, attending seminars, and participating in programmes; doing so will boost your self-confidence.

Listening is another vital aspect of the learning process. Listening is an effective method of learning that will facilitate the growth of your interpersonal skills and relationships. Listening to the experiences and ideas of others can help you gain a deeper understanding of the world and your place within it.

The benefits of being a good listener are numerous, as you can learn from others' mistakes and successes.

I have a story to tell; I struggled with writing many years ago.

I developed a talent for writing, but despite being so intellectually gifted in it, I felt I could not stand out.

I chose coach faith and became her best listener; listening to and practising her podcast was a daily activity for me. I attended her social media life sessions and listened to her audio recordings.

I never commented on anything, but by listening to her I became the best version of myself.

When I am surrounded by brilliant minds, I listen because their discourse is a fully paid course that is being given away for free, and knowledge is essential for the advancement of humanity.

If you want to grow, when you find yourself in the presence of a great mind, learn to speak less and allow them to demonstrate their knowledge, because one thing I have learned is that men will always want to be noticed and recognised, and if you act beneath them, they will try to prove a point to your face in order to gain respect.

You will accomplish a great deal if you choose to listen to them as opposed to attempting to obtain the information they provide during casual conversation.

There is a coach I am familiar with (true identity withheld) She has represented Africa on numerous occasions as a coach for public speaking in Nigeria. I have been a covert student for many years.

This is how I attained success. I started following her on social media, and then I realised that she shares content equivalent to a course wow!!

I began learning every day from her by simply joining the crowd. I participate in her timeline activities, listen to her podcast, and attend her live section. Until she gave me her finest work of literature as a gift.

I acquired all of this by being an attentive listener and a perpetual student. You can perform better if you try.

Mastering a new concept requires time and focus, but don't you wish there was a quicker method? While cramming will not help you learn the material faster in the long run, employing smart and effective learning strategies will. We'll begin with strategies for learning and reviewing material before moving on to lifestyle modifications that can enhance your memory.

Something written down is more likely to be remembered. Pay close attention to the lecture and take notes on the keywords and phrases you hear if you are in class. If you're studying something online or from a book, rephrase what you read in your own words, as this will help you retain the information. This will allow you to recall it more quickly.

If you wanted to learn more about U.S. history, for instance, you could create a timeline of all the significant dates and events. Pay complete attention to your study while taking notes so you don't miss any vital information. Review your notes immediately after taking them and organise them so that they are easier to read again.

Hearing oneself repeat the information aids in retention. Read aloud when studying from a book, the Internet, or your notes. Examine the text slowly to avoid missing anything essential. Try pointing to the words as you read them to help you remember them more effectively. The more often you recite information aloud, the easier it will be to remember it.

If you are attempting to learn a new language, for instance, you should practise pronouncing new vocabulary words and phrases as you acquire them. Because you are actively speaking, you will retain the information better in your long-term memory.

Determine which topics you still need to review by taking a quiz. After reading or studying something, put your knowledge to the test by repeating everything you just learned. Consider writing down the definitions of terms or phrases if you need to recall them rather than looking them up. Make a note of what you have trouble remembering so you can review and rehearse it. You will not waste time concentrating on information you already know well.

For example, if you are testing yourself on a chapter from a textbook, you should summarise the entire chapter in your own words. Then, review the chapter's conclusion for any keywords and attempt to define them.

You can also find numerous online practise exams for the subject you are studying.

Chapter 7 Concluding Considerations

Many Christians are genuinely affected by depression. It can make you feel alone, isolated, and hopeless. Today, depression is on the rise due to the constant barrage of negative news. Many work environments are demanding and do not promote a healthy work-life balance. Our homes are not sanctuaries because they are filled with to-do lists, strife, and arguments with spouses and children. These variables can all contribute to fatigue and depression.

Depression is treatable and need not rule or destroy your life. However, we must be able to identify the signs and symptoms of depression in ourselves and others and know when to seek assistance. There is hope always. A Christian counsellor can help you develop a plan to promote mental and physical health.

## Chapter 4: Depression's Nine Manifestations

Throughout the day, feelings of melancholy or emptiness. Depressed disposition You feel the urge to cry more frequently than usual.

Decreased interest in formerly enjoyable activities, hobbies, or work.

Changes in eating habits, including appetite loss or overeating.

Inability to fall asleep, insomnia, or restless sleep that causes morning fatigue. Need assistance getting out of bed in the morning and/or desire to sleep throughout the day. Fewer calories than usual. Increased physical symptoms may include headaches, digestive disorders, or a rapid heartbeat.

Not functioning normally, agitation, pacing, and slowed speech. Changes that others are beginning to observe.

Feelings of worthlessness or inappropriate or excessive guilt.

Worrying about the past and the unknown future.

A diminished capacity for thought and concentration. Almost constant feelings of indecisiveness.

Fearing the start of a new day or the decisions and responsibilities of life. Considerations that life is not worth living

Recurrent suicidal ideation, with or without specific plans to execute the ideation.

FIVE METHODS TO CONQUER DEPRESSION

Counseling: Counselors can assist you in gaining an objective viewpoint. Find a therapist with expertise in treating depression. A competent counsellor can assist you in developing a personalised plan to combat depression.

Safe Folks: It is essential to have a support network. Being a part of a small group in your church is a great way to connect and find safe, accepting people.

Take Good Care of Yourself: Engage in enjoyable activities, such as walking, being in nature, and listening to music. Exercising has been shown to improve your mood, according to scientific research.

When a depressed or anxious thought enters your mind, turn it into a prayer rather than worrying. "Have no worries about anything." Philippians 4:6. A skilled counsellor can assist you in assessing whether you are viewing the world through a lens of pessimism or optimism.

Relax and Read the Bible: Every night, getting at least 5 to 6 hours of uninterrupted sleep improves your mood. Then, pause and commune with God. Reading the Bible will assist you in ministering to your situation.

Do not demand too much of yourself too quickly. This will only heighten the sense of failure. Instead, initiate small changes and establish attainable objectives. The evaluation of some individuals by a psychiatrist, who can determine if they are candidates for medication, can be beneficial. Often, chemical imbalances in the brain can be the cause of clinical depression. It is not "all in your head." New developments in antidepressants and SSRIs can help you regain your sense of self.

Physical Considerations: Struggle to Exhaustion

We frequently fail to recognise that our spiritual and psychological state is profoundly influenced by our physical circumstances. Sometimes, exhaustion is the cause of depression. In 1 Kings 19, the prophet Elijah, exhausted by his battle with Jezebel and her prophets, is so depressed that he begs God to take his life. God's remedy for Elijah was to eat a healthy meal, rest, and expect to feel better in the morning.

Diet and Exercise: Respecting God's Temple

Diet and exercise can also affect our psychological and spiritual health. The Bible states that the human body is "the temple of God" (1 Corinthians 6:19), and it is regrettable how poorly many of us treat our bodies. I wonder how many of us would experience greater spiritual vitality and happiness if we exercised and ate foods that were beneficial rather than harmful. Large quantities of junk food can induce a temporary high. Nonetheless, the long-term impact on our emotional and psychological health is negative.

Biological Contributions to Chemical Imbalance

Depression is also caused by chemical imbalances in the body. It is difficult to think positively when a chemical imbalance exists. The DNA of a person can trigger chemical reactions that put them in a foul mood. Changes in the female body that accompany menopause can cause severe depression in women. Prayer is a potent instrument, but escaping depression due to a chemical imbalance is unlikely. Those who claim that faith alone is the cure for clinical depression and try to dissuade Christians from seeking medical assistance will only prolong a person's struggle.

In many instances, severe depression lasting more than a few days is biophysically based and requires medical treatment. This is unquestionably true for those with bipolar disorder. A psychiatrist is trained to identify both the physical and psychological causes of depression. Such treatment does not indicate a lack of faith, but rather a willingness to utilise what God has made available to humanity through modern science.

## Chapter 5: When Day-To-Day Difficulties Become Overwhelming

Sometimes people are depressed simply because their jobs are unsatisfying. Employment can dehumanise a person and leave them exhausted and disheartened. Also, personal tragedies of one kind or another can deplete a person's capacity for love. Allow me to quickly add that grief is inevitable and necessary in the face of tragedy and loss, so long as it does not last forever.

### The Effectiveness of Confession in Beginning the Healing Process

A great way to begin the healing process is to admit to others that, despite being a Christian, you experience depressive feelings. Then, ask them to support you, to pray for you, and to assist you in getting out of bed and beginning to do things despite feeling depressed. The most important thing is to begin coping with your depression and moving toward healthy fishing.

Conclusion: Emotions can lead us astray, but God's Word is stable and unchanging. Consequently, we must maintain a strong faith in God and cling to Him even more tightly during trials and temptations. According to the Bible, God will never allow us to face temptations that we cannot withstand (1 Corinthians 10:13).

Although being depressed is not a sin, it is still one's responsibility to respond to the condition, including seeking professional assistance. "Therefore, through Jesus, let us continually offer to God a sacrifice of praise — the fruit of lips that confess his name" (Hebrews 13:15). I am praying for everyone. I hope you enjoy the devotional that follows.

Through exercise, you can divert your attention from negative thoughts.

Exercising is advantageous in every circumstance. Breaking your negative thought patterns and distracting yourself from these thoughts is a simple way to maintain mental stability in a crowd. Whenever you feel that unnecessary negative thoughts are dominating your mind, you can make small hand, foot, arm, shoulder, and neck movements to remain comfortable and reduce the impact of negative thoughts on your mind. Can Do Exercises. Exercises Including Snapping Fingers, Rotating Wrist, Rotating Heel Of Foot, Rotating Neck With Eyes Closed, Rotating Shoulders Clockwise And

Counterclockwise, etc. This type of exercise will be accessible on YouTube.

This calms your mind, breaks your negative thought patterns, improves your focus, and sends a message to those who are paying close attention that you are in a normal state of mind and ready to assist them. Feeling At Home In The Center.

# Chapter 6: What It Takes to Maintain Weight Loss: A Gut-Health-Focused Approach

Remember how in the beginning of this book I discussed my troublesome skin rash and steady weight gain? Initiating a gut healing protocol and way of life was a significant part of the solution, but it was not my first attempt to improve how I appeared and felt.

daily allotment of carbohydrates permitted. Previously, I had consumed cereal, sandwiches, pasta, and desserts. This was such a drastic change for my brain and body that I began to experience intense cravings for the foods I desired. I lacked the wisdom to avoid extreme diet and exercise programmes at the time, and I frequently gave in to cravings and disordered eating patterns. This experience was a significant detour that prevented me from recovering from an eating disorder. When I think back to that time, I recall how other members of my online community swore by eating this way and exercising at such a high intensity for months. I recall how frustrated I was that my results never seemed to materialise, and how my relationship with food regressed into vicious binge-eating and purging cycles that required weeks to recover from.

The common misconception regarding extreme programmes is that discipline alone is sufficient to complete the programme. If you give in to cravings, you feel like a failure and conclude that you lack mental strength and self-control. Attempts to lose weight by drastically reducing calories and food groups induce a stress response in the body. Within twelve to twenty-four hours, the liver and muscle glycogen stores are depleted as the body prepares for starvation mode in response to a diminished energy intake. As this stress continues over the next two days, higher levels of cortisol are released into the bloodstream, causing the body to retain more water and increase bloating. At this point, the body slows down its metabolism in response to what it perceives to be a lack of food or starvation. At three days of starvation, your body prefers to store more fat for energy and begins to break down lean muscle. As discussed throughout this book, excess stress has a negative impact on the gut, increasing the likelihood of leaky gut and bacterial overgrowth. Long-term caloric restriction may also result in nutrient deficiencies, which is a recipe for disaster for your digestive health.

In the meantime, your metabolic rate drastically slows, which decreases your thyroid and adrenaline production. This decrease induces a sense of exhaustion and a general lack of physical and mental energy. The majority of your weight loss after one week has been composed of lean muscle mass. If you continue to restrict your caloric intake, the appetite-stimulating hormone ghrelin will accumulate in your system, making it much easier to binge eat. Your disposition will suffer, and you will be preoccupied with food constantly.

Once you decide to stop dieting, you will likely start consuming foods that were off-limits during your diet, and your body will begin to store fat to replenish its energy reserves. The body's fat cells remember previous starvation, and the body's original fat level can be reached more quickly after an extreme diet. Typically, the amount of fat increases over time. 1

If crash diets are ineffective, what alternatives exist? If your objective is to lose weight, you must adopt the mindset of a long-game player. The focus of a crash diet is not learning how to be healthy and live as the person you aspire to be. Instead, you become preoccupied with achieving your objective as quickly as possible, under the illusion that you will be happy once you do so. This is false, and any programme or solution that promotes it is dishonest and encourages short-term thinking. We have been sold the short-term, quick-results lie for far too long, and we no longer believe it. We know on some level that we require a shift from short-term to long-term thinking. When you successfully reframe your weight loss efforts as a long-term endeavour, you will discover that the strategy you commit to is sustainable, mindful, and a slow burn toward your goal. Abandoning the "all or nothing" or "on and off the waggon" mentality will do more than reduce your body fat and boost your confidence; it will also extinguish the smouldering fires of inflammation and stress within you.

You'll be able to implement strategies at a pace that works for you, allowing you to lose weight sustainably while maintaining a healthy gut and good hormone levels. My only hope is that you are able to see through the deceptive marketing tactics of businesspeople and corporations looking to make a quick buck off of you as a consumer who sincerely wants to change your life, and that you agree with a healthy lifestyle involving the power of long-term thinking that will produce lasting results. What if you could reach a point where you do not regain the weight you have lost, plus more? That is the objective, correct? It becomes useful to view it in this manner: Which of the two choices listed below would you select?

- Attaining the desired results in eight weeks, but realising how difficult it will be to maintain the diet and exercise regimen at this level of intensity. You decide to pause and take a break, but you don't wish to restart the current plan. You become disheartened and revert to poorer habits than before, thereby diminishing your overall health.

- Achieving the desired results in two to six months, while allowing your body to adapt at a reasonable rate, so that the positive changes you've made become part of your routine and are easy to maintain. The lifestyle changes you have made have improved your gut health, metabolic health, immune system, and cardiovascular health.

I DON'T KNOW ABOUT YOU, but the second option sounds significantly more long-term viable. Even if I felt uncomfortable about my weight or the way my clothes fit, I know I would be much less likely to revert to unhealthy behaviours such as crash dieting or restricting food. My brain would be much more likely to become aware of this, be equipped to make better decisions, make a minor course correction, and continue on if it were healthy and well-nourished.

Even if your objective is not weight loss, adopting a long-term perspective will always yield superior answers, solutions, and outcomes in everything you undertake.

Here is the news I've been building up to the entire time. What is the secret to losing weight while maintaining health? Follow these steps in conjunction with one another.

Section Two

## Chapter 7: Making the Choice for Recovery — The Path to Healing

Healing is a difficult process for everyone; it is healthy and a good thing to do, but that does not mean it is free of pain and difficulties. Consider a severe wound on the palm of your hand. There will be days when the scab appears, days when the scab is itchy, times when the wound may become infected despite your best efforts, and days when the wound is painful, red, and swollen.

Understanding that the trauma you have experienced has left you with emotional wounds that are deeper and more extensive than you realise is an important part of the healing process. It will take a long time for these wounds to heal, and any difficulties, pain, or suffering you endure are a part of your recovery. As part of your metaphorical treatment, therapy and confronting trauma will alleviate your red-hot irritation, which can fester if left untreated.

Only when you choose to suppress traumatic emotions is there a real risk that the side effects will infect your life.

As discussed in section one, C-PTSD is accompanied by a variety of symptoms that can negatively impact your life. You may even subconsciously self-sabotage because, on some level, your traumatic experience tells you that you do not deserve happiness or success.

These ideologies are all false. You deserve happiness regardless of what has occurred or what your thoughts tell you. You are deserving of the success you seek. You can be loved, prosperous, and peaceful. You are already incredible and must learn to appreciate yourself.

Long-term trauma causes our brains to become clouded with uncertainty, doubt, and confusion. Due to the traumatised state of our brains, it is difficult to see things as they truly are. We truly view the world through the hazy lens of past events. When in fact, if we can take that step into the light, even if we initially see only a sliver of it, we can heal ourselves and discover a different type of inner strength that will elevate us.

This section will discuss your relationship difficulties and provide a more comprehensive explanation of C-PTSD symptoms, as well as healing exercises. It will direct you toward a decision and provide you with strategies to continue your journey when it becomes too challenging or painful.

You deserve the best life possible. You are entitled to obtain your desires. You do not have to be defined by the trauma you experience; you can regain control and discover your resilience.

# Chapter 8: Preserving and Improving Your Mental Health

While seeking professional assistance and developing coping skills and strategies can be helpful in managing anxiety and stress, it is also essential to maintain and strengthen your mental health on an ongoing basis. You can establish a solid foundation for coping with anxiety and stress by incorporating self-care practises and building a supportive network.

The Importance of Self-Care in the Management of Anxiety and Stress: Self-care is an essential component of managing anxiety and stress. By attending to your physical and emotional needs, you can increase your resilience and enhance your overall health.

Consider the following as examples of self-care behaviours:

Regular physical activity can aid in reducing anxiety and stress and enhancing your mood.

2.Sleep: Adequate sleep is essential for maintaining mental health. Aim for seven to nine hours of sleep nightly.

3.Nutrition: A healthy diet can support mental health and decrease anxiety and stress. Aim for a variety of fruits, vegetables, whole grains, and lean proteins in your diet.

4.Relaxation: Incorporating relaxation techniques into your daily routine, such as meditation or deep breathing, can help reduce anxiety and stress.

Engaging in enjoyable activities, such as hobbies or spending time with family and friends, can help you relax and reduce anxiety and stress.

Strategies for Building and Maintaining Mental Health Aside from self-care practises, there are additional strategies for building and maintaining mental health:

1.Seek support: Creating a network of supportive friends, family members, and professionals can be beneficial for coping with anxiety and stress. Being surrounded by supportive individuals can give you a sense of belonging and help you feel less alone.

Mindfulness, or the practise of being in the present moment, can help you become more conscious of your thoughts and emotions and reduce anxiety and stress.

It is essential to find balance in your life and avoid overextending yourself. Make time for self-care and relaxation, and avoid accepting more responsibilities than you can handle.

4.Seek assistance when necessary: If you are unable to manage your anxiety and stress, do not be afraid to seek assistance. It is acceptable to ask for assistance when you need it.

The Importance of Social Support in Anxiety and Stress Management Social support is crucial in anxiety and stress management. Having a network of people on whom you can rely can reduce anxiety and stress and improve your overall health. Among the ways to build a network of support are:

Spend time with your friends and family, or join a group or club that shares your interests.

Consider seeking the assistance of a therapist or other mental health professional if you are having difficulty building a supportive network on your own.

There are numerous online resources, such as support groups and forums, that can provide a sense of community and support for coping with anxiety and stress.

It's normal to encounter setbacks and relapses when coping with anxiety and stress. It is important to be kind to yourself and to remember that ups and downs are normal. It is essential, if you experience a setback or relapse, to:

Try to identify any triggers or warning signs that may have contributed to the setback or relapse. This can help you develop strategies to prevent future setbacks and relapses by enhancing your comprehension of your anxiety and stress.

When you are struggling, do not be afraid to reach out to your supportive network or a professional for assistance. Having someone to confide in and lean on can provide reassurance and reduce anxiety and stress.

3.Practice self-care: Remind yourself to practise self-care by engaging in activities that help you relax and reduce anxiety and stress. This may include physical activity, adequate rest, and participation in enjoyable activities.

4.Review your coping skills and strategies and try new ones if you are having difficulty managing your anxiety and stress. By having a variety of coping skills and strategies at your disposal, you will be better able to face challenges as they arise.

5. Consider seeking professional assistance: If you are unable to manage your anxiety and stress on your own, consider seeking professional assistance. They can help you develop a plan for managing your symptoms and preventing setbacks and relapses in the future.

You can overcome setbacks and continue working to maintain and improve your mental health if you are patient and kind to yourself, and if you seek assistance when necessary. Remember that progress takes time, and that it is essential to be consistent and persistent in your efforts to manage anxiety and stress.

# Chapter 9: Simple Methods To Fight Stress And Anxiety

How can we alleviate our stress? With the aid of exercise, a healthy diet, time management, and sleep, we can manage stressful situations in our lives. Mindfulness practises and exercises are also beneficial. Although managing chronic stress is more challenging, you should focus on the things you can control and cultivate a support network. In addition, understanding how our bodies respond to stress may help us decide whether to seek assistance. If you frequently feel overwhelmed, you don't have to simply endure it; instead, seek assistance from a mental health professional who can help you regain your equilibrium.

Numerous people frequently experience daily anxiety and stress. Everyday stresses, such as those associated with work, family, health, and finances, can frequently result in elevated levels of stress.

Additionally, variables such as heredity, social support, coping mechanisms, and personality type influence a person's susceptibility to stress, so some individuals are more susceptible to stress than others.

Chronic stress from daily life should be reduced as much as possible for one's general health. This is due to the fact that chronic stress is detrimental to health and increases the likelihood of developing heart disease, anxiety disorders, and depression.

Do not speak with your fears.

Your anxieties converse with you. Do not respond to their comments. Consider God.

This is frequently difficult because our imaginations are a good hiding place for anxiety. They appear so plausible, which makes them emotionally engaging to contemplate. Anxieties are capable of impersonation, frequently adopting the form of recognisable individuals. These enemies are among the most difficult to combat.

These people may be relatives, friends, churchgoers, coworkers, acquaintances, or people we know only by reputation in the real world. They may be people with whom we have a strained relationship, with whom we disagree on an issue, or against whom we are at odds. It could be people we fear will misunderstand us, fail us, see our weakness or ignorance, confront us with the painful truth, or whose sin we fear is an indication of serious spiritual issues. They could also be individuals whose influence we fear will harm a family member or our church.

Whatever they actually are, something about them makes us uncomfortable.

Then, our concern may manifest as that individual in our thoughts and initiate a dialogue with us. When it makes provocative statements to us, we respond. Before we realise it, we have been embroiled in a protracted dispute in our minds, which has sparked all manner of evil emotions and led us to feel and think negatively of the actual person. However, we have not even spoken with them. We have sinned both by succumbing to faithless anxiety and by failing to love that individual. We've addressed our anxiety.

God provides no instructions in the Bible on how to combat anxiety. It's never successful. Scripture simply instructs us to pray about our concerns and have faith that God will provide for them all (1 Peter 5:7; Philippians 4:6–7, 19).

Not All Panic Is Bad

There is justifiable anxiety, such as that experienced by Jesus in the Garden of Gethsemane (Matthew 26:38–39), by Paul for the churches (2 Corinthians 11:28), and by parents over the potentially harmful influences their children may encounter in the outside world. If Christians in the United States are "worried" about the acceptance and institutionalisation of evil, they are not necessarily sinful. The Bible gives us good reason to fear and be concerned about the actual or potential harm that wickedness may cause to lives of immeasurable value.

The Bible instructs us to entrust our cares to God and rely on him to provide for us.

When we, like Jesus and Paul, transform our fear-driven concerns into prayer requests, intertwining them with gratitude for the blessings we've received from God and all the promises he's made (2 Peter 1:4), and give them to God, that is what prevents them from becoming sinful. God receives glory as the all-sufficient, abundantly generous object of our faith (2 Corinthians 9:8), and we receive the joys of knowing the heart- and mind-guarding peace that surpasses understanding before we receive our request (Philippians 4:6-7) as well as the ultimate provision we require.

Prayer is the key to avoiding the trap of immoral anxiety. Avoid listening to your worries and responding to them. Be especially wary of anxiety that disguises itself. God is the only one who can guarantee that everything will work out in the end, so pray to him and place all your "what-if" concerns in his hands.

The Lord will defend you.

Today, I wanted to focus on a spiritual conflict that many parents and leaders of children's ministries may be experiencing. To say that the current era is difficult would be a gross understatement. The majority of us face a variety of personal struggles. In actuality, it is nearly impossible to properly instil in our children a sense of trust in God if they consistently observe us displaying fear and anxiety. Children are exposed to such events. I am able to say this because I have personal experience with it. I am occasionally guilty of not peacefully upholding the faith that I so fervently preach.

I've recently been reading through the Book of Exodus, and Exodus 14 has me completely enthralled. God tells Moses to lead the Israelites out of Canaan and toward the Red Sea. Moses had just led the Israelites out of Egypt. This would convince Pharaoh, whose heart God is said to have hardened once more, that the Israelites were simply lost and confused. As Pharaoh's army pursued them, it became evident that God's chosen people, the descendants of Israel, were doomed. They cried out to Moses and the Lord that it would have been preferable for them to remain slaves in Egypt rather than perish in the desert.

Moses reassured his people that the Lord would fight on their behalf as he remained faithful to the vision God had given him. (14) Exodus

The Israelites were not steadfast in their conviction that they could once again place their trust in the same God who had led them through so many obstacles. They questioned the Lord and believed that He had abandoned them.

We are already aware of the story's conclusion, and God certainly has a plan in mind. It was unclear whether he wanted them to alter their course or not. It wasn't clear until the very last instant. But God was trustworthy.

At this point, can you identify with the Israelites' scepticism? I can. Do you feel anxious about the unpredictability of life as you roam the streets today? Have you lost sight of God's blessings for you? You claim to have surrendered it to God, but have you truly let it go?

God has promised to take care of whatever is causing you anxiety, concern, or fear if you are emotionally, spiritually, or even physically exhausted from fighting a battle on your own. Rest under our Lord's protection. He is prepared to save you!

# Chapter 10: Enhancing Productivity And Maintaining A Healthy Work-Life Balance Through Emotional Mastery At Work

motional mastery at work may be described as the capacity to control and regulate one's emotions in a manner that allows for optimum productivity and a good work-life balance.

This is an essential ability to have in today's fast-paced, high-stress work environment, as it helps people to handle the difficulties and expectations of the job with perseverance and grace.

There are many major tactics that people may utilize to achieve emotional mastery at work:

*Practice mindfulness:* Mindfulness is the discipline of focusing one's attention to the present moment, without judgment.

It entails being aware of and embracing one's ideas, emotions, and bodily sensations in a non-reactive manner. When we are attentive, we are better able to manage our emotions and react to difficulties in a more considered and effective way.

*Set boundaries:* Establishing clear boundaries between work and personal life is vital for establishing a good work-life balance.

This involves putting limitations on the amount of time and energy we commit to work, as well as being clear about what we are and are not prepared to undertake in the workplace.

*Take care of your physical and mental health:* Our physical and mental health are tightly interrelated. To retain emotional control at work, it is crucial to emphasize self-care by obtaining adequate sleep, eating a good diet, and participating in regular physical exercise. It is also crucial to practice stress-management strategies, such as deep breathing, meditation, or yoga, to assist decrease anxiety and increase mental well-being.

*Communicate effectively:* Being able to speak clearly and effectively is key for managing emotions at work. This involves listening attentively to others, being forceful in expressing our own needs and limits, and seeking out help when required.

*Cultivate a growth mentality:* A growth mindset is the concept that we can learn, grow, and change through effort and experience. By adopting a growth mindset, we may approach obstacles and setbacks as opportunities for learning and progress, rather than considering them as personal failures.

This allows us to stay resilient and motivated, even when presented with unpleasant conditions.

Emotional mastery at work is a vital ability that helps people to negotiate the demands and difficulties of the job with perseverance and grace. By practicing mindfulness, establishing boundaries, taking care of physical and mental health, communicating effectively, and creating a growth mindset, we may enhance productivity and maintain a good work-life balance.

# Chapter 11: Differences Between Bipolar Disorder And Anxiety Disorders

Bipolar disorder and anxiety disorders are both mental illnesses that can significantly impair a person's daily functioning. While both diseases involve mood and behaviour changes, there are fundamental differences between them.

Bipolar disorder is characterised by extreme mood swings ranging from manic or hypomanic episodes to intense bouts of depression. These mood swings can be intense and sudden, and they can last for days or weeks. People with bipolar disorder may experience alterations in their energy levels, sleep patterns, concentration, appetite, and weight. During manic episodes, they may also engage in risky or impulsive behaviour, such as spending sprees or reckless driving.

In contrast, anxiety disorders are characterised by excessive anxiety and dread that can impair a person's daily functioning. Anxiety disorders may consist of, among others, generalised anxiety disorder, social anxiety disorder, and panic disorder. People with anxiety disorders may experience both physical and mental symptoms, including sweating, heart palpitations, and difficulty breathing, as well as irritability, difficulty focusing, and difficulty sleeping. Unlike bipolar disorder, anxiety disorders rarely involve significant mood shifts.

Therapy is a significant difference between bipolar disorder and anxiety disorders. Bipolar disorder is frequently treated with a combination of medications, such as mood stabilisers and antipsychotics, and psychotherapy to address underlying causes and assist with symptom management. In contrast, anxiety disorders are typically treated with cognitive-behavioral therapy and pharmaceuticals such as antidepressants or anti-anxiety medications.

Prevalence is another distinction between the two diseases. Bipolar disorder affects approximately 2.8% of the population, whereas anxiety disorders affect approximately 18.1%. Bipolar disorder is also more prevalent in adulthood, whereas anxiety disorders can manifest at any age.

Although bipolar disorder and anxiety disorders are distinct diagnoses, co-occurrence is possible. In reality, those with bipolar disorder are more likely to experience anxiety issues, and those with anxiety disorders are more likely to develop bipolar disorder. This overlap highlights the importance of seeking professional treatment if mood swings or disruptive behaviour are interfering with your daily life. It is possible to manage bipolar disorder and anxiety disorders and live a productive and meaningful life with proper treatment and support.

## Prevalence

Bipolar disorder and anxiety disorders are two of the most prevalent mental health conditions affecting people worldwide. There may be some similarities, but they are distinct syndromes with distinct prevalence rates and causes.

Bipolar disorder, also referred to as manic-depressive disorder, is a condition characterised by extreme mood swings ranging from mania to depression. Bipolar disorder is approximately 1 percent prevalent in the general population, with an average onset age of 25 years.

In contrast, anxiety disorders are a group of mental health conditions characterised by excessive anxiety and fear. Anxiety disorders include generalised anxiety disorder, social anxiety disorder, and panic disorder. Anxiety disorders are significantly more prevalent than bipolar disorder, with an estimated prevalence of approximately 18%. The average onset age for anxiety disorders is approximately 21 years old.

There are a number of important distinctions between bipolar disorder and anxiety disorders, which contribute to their distinct prevalence rates. One of the primary differences between diseases is their causes. Bipolar disorder is believed to be caused by a combination of genetic and environmental factors. On the other hand, it is believed that anxiety disorders are caused by a combination of genetic, environmental, and psychological factors.

The severity of the symptoms is a further distinction between the two illnesses. Bipolar disorder is a severe condition with potentially fatal complications if left untreated. On the other hand, anxiety disorders are frequently less severe, but they can still have a significant impact on an individual's quality of life.

A lack of knowledge and understanding regarding bipolar disorder is one of the fundamental causes for the frequency difference between bipolar illness and anxiety disorders. Many people may be unaware that they have bipolar disorder because they cannot recognise the symptoms or do not seek treatment. This misunderstanding may contribute to the fact that bipolar disorder is less prevalent than anxiety disorders.

It is essential to understand the differences between bipolar disorder and anxiety disorders in order to provide appropriate treatment and support to those affected by these conditions. If you or someone you know is afflicted with any of these conditions, it is crucial to seek the assistance of a mental health professional. Managing and living well with either of these conditions is possible with the proper treatment and support.

Age Of Onset

Due to their overlapping symptoms, bipolar disorder and anxiety disorders are distinct mental health conditions that are frequently misdiagnosed. The onset age is a significant distinction between the two, however.

Bipolar disorder typically manifests in late adolescence or early adulthood. The National Institute of Mental Health reports that the average age of onset for bipolar disorder is 25. However, it is extremely uncommon to diagnose bipolar disorder in individuals as young as 15 or as old as 40.

On the other hand, anxiety disorders can manifest at any age throughout a person's life. Although anxiety disorders can manifest in infancy, they are more often diagnosed in adulthood. According to the National Institute of Mental Health, the average age of onset for anxiety disorders is 21.

There are numerous potential causes for the differences in onset age between bipolar disorder and anxiety disorders. Bipolar disorder is typically initiated by hormonal fluctuations that occur during adolescence and early adulthood. This may explain why bipolar disorder is more likely to be diagnosed in this age range.

The existence of environmental stresses may also contribute to the disparity in onset age. Anxiety disorders can be caused by stress, including work-related stress, family problems, and financial difficulties. These stresses can manifest at any age, leading to the development of anxiety disorders.

It is essential to remember that the onset age of bipolar disorder and anxiety disorders can vary significantly between individuals. Some adolescents may develop bipolar disorder, while others may not be diagnosed until much later in life. Similarly, some people may develop anxiety issues as children, while others may not experience symptoms until later in life.

It is also important to note that bipolar disorder and anxiety disorders can occur simultaneously. It is uncommon for individuals with bipolar disorder to also exhibit anxiety symptoms. This may make it more difficult to identify and effectively treat both diseases.

The age of onset is a significant distinction between bipolar disorder and anxiety disorders. Bipolar disorder typically manifests in late adolescence or early adulthood, whereas anxiety disorders can appear at any age. Understanding this distinction may be necessary for the proper identification and treatment of these diseases.

## Duration And Course Of Illness

In order to distinguish between bipolar and anxiety disorders, duration and disease duration are crucial characteristics. Bipolar disorder is characterised by extreme mood swings, ranging from periods of extreme euphoria or mania to extreme depression. These mood swings, or episodes, may persist for weeks or even months. The duration and progression of bipolar disorder may vary considerably from person to person. Some individuals may experience only a few episodes, while others may endure a large number of repeated episodes.

In contrast, anxiety disorders are characterised by excessive and persistent fear in response to particular events or stimuli. The duration and course of anxiety disorders can also vary considerably between individuals. Some individuals may experience anxiety that lasts only a few weeks or months, whereas others may suffer from chronic anxiety that lasts for years.

It is essential to emphasise that bipolar and anxiety disorders can significantly impact a person's daily life and functioning. However, the therapeutic options available for these diseases varied considerably. Bipolar disorder is typically treated with medication and psychotherapy, whereas anxiety disorders are frequently treated with medication, therapy, and changes in lifestyle.

Additionally, it is important to note that bipolar disorder and anxiety disorders can sometimes co-occur, meaning that a person can suffer from both conditions simultaneously. In such cases, treatment options may need to be modified to address both diseases simultaneously.

In conclusion, the duration and progression of bipolar and anxiety disorders can vary considerably between individuals. Individuals with any of these diseases must collaborate closely with a healthcare professional to develop a treatment plan tailored to their specific needs and circumstances.

Those with bipolar or anxiety disorders can learn to control their symptoms and lead productive lives if they receive the appropriate treatment.

# Chapter 12: Key Strategies To De-Stress The Mind

The mind is an excellent instrument for contemplating, conceptualising, observing, and assimilating information. Stress is inevitable when the instrument becomes the Master.

Your mind is like a computer in that it is full of data. Additionally, it provides a management application for such data. Using certain perceptions and interpretations you learned as a young child, your mind shapes the information it takes in. Unless you decide to alter it, your mind is governed by the programming from your upbringing.

To de-stress, it is necessary to be conscious of and update these early ideas.

Who you believe you are (self-concept) and who you believe you ought to be are formed by what we hear, see, and experience as infants (self-ideal).

The self-images that provide the foundation for self-esteem, self-worth, and self-determination — the freedom to make independent decisions — are not ones that you deliberately choose. You will undoubtedly fall short of this unattainable self-ideal, and it is distressing to consider that you have little autonomy over your choices.

Fight, flight, and freeze are the three primary types of distress responses.

Do you tend to withdraw, hide, and absorb stress through passivity or depression? Is it to react violently, attack, and express stress externally through dominance, anxiety, or aggression? Or do you become immobile and trapped? In both instances, the fundamental issues and solutions are identical.

The advice that follows is straightforward, reasonable, and actionable. However, implementation may be challenging.

1 Sort out your stresses.
Understanding which aspects of life you have control over and which you do not is the key to mental relaxation. Nothing external to yourself is under your control. The things within you are entirely under your control. Considering how people typically behave, this does not appear revolutionary. If you're like most people, you attribute your stress to external factors and spend the majority of your time and energy attempting to manage the uncontrollable ineffectively. Time (not enough, past, future), nature (disease, age, death, weather), and other individuals are a few of the

uncontrollables on the list (what they think, feel, say, do).

Stress is alleviated when you focus your time and energy on YOU, understanding how you think and feel, and deciding what is most important to you. YOU are the only individual over whom you have absolute control and the ability to shape your life.

By categorising what you can and cannot manage, it may be easier to decide where to focus your attention. Although the conditioned mind (ego) finds it challenging to accept change, it enjoys structure. The mind is more receptive to new ideas when they are presented in a logical manner.

2 Make your selection first

Only decisions can be made in the present moment. The future has not yet arrived, and the past is nothing more than a memory. Make prudent decisions by drawing from past experience. The decisions we make now have an impact on the future. The most effective action you can take right now is to make a deliberate choice regarding your actions. Each day contains a fixed amount of time. You are responsible for deciding what to do with it. Prioritizing what is most important to you makes it easier to identify tasks that must be delegated or eliminated from the "to-do" list.

When you accept responsibility for your current actions and are realistic about what you can accomplish, life becomes much simpler, less stressful, and more fruitful. Today, you should be mindful of your decisions and attentive to how they affect the outcomes.

You are the only person who can affect your decisions. It is also possible to decide to do nothing. By making deliberate decisions, you can determine the course and fulfilment of your life. Your choices influence those around you, but not in a controlling manner. The first step toward altering the world begins within oneself.

A change in one part of the whole has an effect on the whole.

3 Examine your mental state

What is your mental reaction to this information? Fight means to oppose and seek logical errors, flight means to divert attention away from the text, and freeze means to be uncertain as to what action to take. The mind is resistant to changing established beliefs. Observe its response. This aspect of the conditioned mind, also known as the inner bully or critic, is a potent impediment to making life changes.

As a child, your mind began to formulate ideas about how to stay safe in the world. The conditioned mind (ego) only cares about its own survival and safety. It becomes frightening when you choose not to live your life according to traditional, "safe" guidelines. Similar to a parent, it continues to dictate what you should and should not do and harshly evaluate your performance. Despite the importance of the brain's survival mechanisms, you are no longer an infant or child. Fight, flight, and freeze are only partially effective relationship and adult life management strategies.

Which phrases does your mind use to bind you to the past? What is the pitch of the voice? What individual's voice is that? Mom, Dad, or someone else? Note your observations in a journal. You may find hints in your diary regarding the pattern or "law" that continues to influence your decisions. One of mine was, "If you speak your mind, no one will like you." Then, I would continually reflect on what I had said and evaluate its potential outcomes. This rule was time-consuming, damaging to relationships, and counterproductive in the workplace; it was intended to "protect" me from criticism.

You are not made by your ideas. Your intellect was designed to aid you in decision-making, not to dictate it. Although your initial unconscious programme kept you safe as a child, you must update it intentionally so that it can assist you as a strong, capable adult. Understanding how the mind functions restores your control over your life.

4 Stop, give up, and replace your inner critic

Whenever you hear that inner voice spewing shoulds, shouldn'ts, or judgements, take action to silence it (good or negative).

Every inner voice is different. If it is hostile or violent, you should intervene with force. You could use more creative language, ponder, or shout "Stop!" The tone of my inner pundit is both insightful and manipulative. I say "Thank you for sharing" and then end the conversation immediately.

Abandon the notion of what you "should" be. None of the individuals comprising this composite lead your specific life. When you hear the words "should" or "should not," you may want to ask, "Who came up with that?" Recognize that only a few natural rules exist. All other things are human inventions. Some beliefs facilitate social interaction. Choose those you wish to keep and discard the remainder.

Replace the preceding rules with those that provide support. In response to my earlier statement, "If you express your true beliefs, people will not like you," I say, "By sharing my truth, others may connect with me and connect with their truth."

Your conditioned images are not indicative of who you are or what you "should" be. As if you were a child, they are operating programmes that control your priceless life unconsciously. Your mental operating system is comparable to that of a computer. The course of life is perpetually in flux.

How will your computer serve you if you never delete old files to make room for new ones or update the operating system to keep up with the latest technological advances? To assist you in consciously choosing the life you want in the present, you must constantly monitor and update your mind.

These mental relaxation techniques will alter your perspective and grant you greater choice control. Sort the things you have control over (within you) from the things you do not (outside of you), pay attention to the things you have control over, and notice how uncomfortable it is for your mind to be present in the moment. Then, stop, drop, and replace any negative self-criticism and judgement based on conditioned beliefs.

USING MANTRAS

If you can master the use of mantras, you will be able to master the technique of having a calm mind. Mantras may help you remain more focused on achieving your goals, thereby increasing your overall productivity.

What is a mantra then? In the end, a mantra is a sound energy. The sound produced may be a syllable, a phrase, or a collection of words that, when chanted or sung repeatedly, can induce a specific change in a person. They may have an effect on a person's mind and body, among other characteristics. When you speak any word, you may feel a physical vibration if you give it some thought. If you are aware of the vibration's effect, eventually it will begin to have significance in relation to the effects of repeatedly saying that phrase.

Mantras are utilised in numerous languages and religions. Ave Maria, for instance, is a well-known Christian prayer recited worldwide. Another well-known mantra is the Tibetan mantra. Mani Padme Hung People hum this phrase to promote international harmony.

Everyone is aware that life can be stressful and demanding at times. Finding 10 minutes per day to relax may be difficult for you. What then can you do? However, you may try reciting some mantras. A mantra is an individualised meditation technique. Utilizing mantras as a form of focused meditation may assist you in making numerous positive changes.

Selecting and remembering your mantra is the initial step you must take. Mantras may be conventional or esoteric. You may utilise commonly employed sounds such as Aum. If you feel uncomfortable using a slogan, simply create your own, such as "I want to be more communicative with others." or "I want to achieve all of my goals." Even making up your own words is acceptable if they have significance to you.

The second step is to find a quiet, distraction-free location where you can use your mantra. Therefore, you will need to allocate some time for that. Just five to ten minutes per day is all that is required for effective mantra usage.

Now, please close your eyes and take a seat in a comfortable position. The time has come to begin reciting your mantra. As you recite your mantra, take a few slow, deep breaths and allow all of the stress and irritation in your body and mind to vanish.

After five to ten minutes of chanting, you may chant for an additional five minutes to fully absorb the mantra you've been meditating on. This will assist you in releasing the stress that has been weighing on your mind all day.

## Chapter 13: Anxiety Disorders

Susan awakens every night, a few hours after falling asleep, with a tightness in her throat, a racing heart, vertigo, and the fear that she is about to die. She is shivering uncontrollably, but cannot pinpoint the cause. After

She has repeatedly paced the floor of her living room at night in an attempt to regain composure. She eventually decides to see a doctor about the possibility that something is wrong with her heart.

Cindy, a medical secretary, has been experiencing panic attacks in confined public areas, just like Susan. She is terrified of what others will think of her if she loses control, as well as her own loss of control.

The presence of her ex-boyfriend has rendered her unwilling to leave the 7-Eleven near her residence. She has previously had to abruptly end dates at restaurants or theatres because she needed to get home. Now she questions her ability to retain her position. She has been forcing herself to go to the office, but after a few minutes of chitchat with her coworkers, she begins to feel as though she might snap. She has forced herself to go to work. She is compelled to leave her home immediately.

Steve, a software engineer in a position of responsibility, fears that he will never advance in his career because he cannot effectively contribute in team settings. Even attending the meetings, let alone contributing his ideas, is almost too much for him at this point.

His manager had asked him the day prior if he was available to present on the portion of the large project that fell under his purview. When Steve realised he was unable to communicate, his anxiety levels spiked and he became mute. He stumbled out of the room, muttering to himself that he would inform his boss of the presentation by the following day. During moments of solitude, he contemplated quitting his job.

Mike has been experiencing an unusual phobia for the past few months, but he is too embarrassed to tell anyone, including his wife, about it. Frequent panic attacks occur while he is driving because he fears hitting and killing a person or animal. Even though there is no audible "thud" to indicate that something of this nature has occurred, he feels compelled to make a U-turn and retrace his steps in order to be certain. In fact, he must retrace his steps three or four times to ensure that nothing untoward has occurred, as he has recently developed a severe phobia of potentially colliding with someone. Mike is a highly educated and successful professional, so his need for constant checking embarrasses him. He believes everyone is aware of it. Momentarily, he wondered if he had lost his mind.

Susan, Cindy, Steve, and Michael all experience anxiety. However, this is not your usual concern. What they are experiencing is fundamentally distinct from the "normal" anxiety that people experience in response to day-to-day stresses and can be summarised as follows: Initially, they have difficulty controlling their anxiety. Each circumstance renders the protagonist helpless and unable to alter the course of events. When people feel helpless, they are more prone to worry. The second problem is that the anxious feelings make everyday life difficult. Susan is experiencing disturbed sleep. Cindy and Steve's employment may be at risk. And Mike can no longer drive as effectively and rapidly as he once did. The actions of Susan, Cindy, Steve, and Mike are typical of those with panic disorder, agoraphobia, social phobia, and obsessive-compulsive disorder. Subsequent subsections of this chapter will provide detailed descriptions of the symptoms and causes that distinguish the various anxiety disorders. However, before we dive in, I'd like you to consider the underlying theme that connects them all. How much does anxiety result from its underlying factors?

In order to gain a better understanding of the dynamics of anxiety, it may be useful to consider both what it is and what it is not. Anxiety, for example, can be distinguished from dread by a number of distinct characteristics. Generally, a person's fear is focused on a single object or situation when they are terrified.

Entity or condition placed on the outside, the occurrence of this dreadful scenario is frequently not inconceivable. It's possible that you're afraid of missing a deadline, performing poorly on an exam, falling behind on your bills, or being rejected by someone you'd like to impress very much. On the other hand, when experiencing anxiety, it can be difficult to pinpoint the source of one's fear. Anxiety is characterised by an inward rather than an outward concentration.

It appears to be a response to a threat that is unclear, distant, or not present at all. It is possible that you fear "losing control" of yourself or the situation you find yourself in. Anxiety can also manifest as a pervasive apprehension that "something terrible is about to occur." It is at once a physiological, behavioural, and psychological response. Anxiety can cause a variety of physiological responses in the body, such as a rapid heartbeat, tense muscles, an upset stomach, dry lips, and profuse sweating, to name a few. At the level of behaviour, it may impair your ability to act, express yourself, or deal with certain everyday situations.

From a psychological perspective, anxiety can be defined as the subjective experience of apprehension and unease.

In its most extreme form, it may cause you to feel alienated from yourself and give you the impression that you will die or lose your mind.

The fact that anxiety can impact you not only physically, but also behaviorally and psychologically, has significant implications for your efforts to improve your health. A comprehensive treatment plan for anxiety disorders must incorporate interventions on all three levels to achieve the following:

Reduce physiologic reactivity

2. Eliminate avoidance behaviour.

Change the interpretations you have in your mind, also known as "self-talk," that place you in a state of tension and anxiety. Anxiety can manifest in a variety of ways and at a broad

spectrum of intensities. Anxiety can range from a fleeting sensation of unease to a full-blown panic attack characterised by heart palpitations, dizziness, and fear. Both free-floating anxiety and spontaneous panic episodes, which are more severe forms of free-floating anxiety, refer to the same condition. If you are experiencing four or more of the following symptoms concurrently, you may be experiencing a panic attack rather than an episode of unfocused anxiety. A panic attack is caused by the simultaneous appearance of four or more of the following symptoms.*
Uneasy and shallow breaths

# Chapter 14: Types Of Assistance To Consider

There are four levels of professionals, each with a distinct function. You can choose one based on your condition (as diagnosed by your general practitioner (GP)), your needs, and your desire. It is not as if one is superior to another based on their credentials and type of treatment. Professionals are available to assist you to the best of their abilities. Simply put, what may work for me may not work for you. Similar to how your parents may have different parenting styles, you never know when you will require more of whom. Similarly, you may require different types of assistance at various times. Therefore, it is preferable to consult a physician regarding the type of treatment required or suggested for you.

1) GENERAL PRACTITIONER: Visit your family physician! They have been treating you for some time and are familiar with your physical patterns. Now, since you already have a connection with them, it can work both ways: it may make it easier for you to share your feelings, emotions, and symptoms, or it may prevent you from doing so. Regardless of the circumstance, they would be your best initial option. Depending on their diagnosis and severity, they can initially attempt treatment with body-supporting medications such as vitamins, probiotics, etc. (Probiotic because there is a direct link between the gut and the brain) to assist the body in healing itself. Or administer a mild medication. Otherwise, they may refer you to a mental health professional.

2) COUNSELOR: They are focused on identifying and implementing solutions for your current issues. As part of their treatment, they guide you through your current crisis and assist you in making a healthy decision while discussing your emotions and concerns. These are non-pharmaceutical, brief treatments in which the therapist simply listens to your issues and makes suggestions for overcoming them. The majority of the time, however, they are only concerned with the current obstacles and not with historical psychological profiling, past experiences, or deep-seated traumas. There are numerous types of school, marriage, substance abuse, and mental health counsellors, depending on their respective areas of expertise.

3) CLINICAL PSYCHOLOGIST: Psychologists typically employ a variety of therapies to treat their patients. They may collaborate with a psychiatrist

regarding medication, but only if necessary. To diagnose a patient's mental health condition, they analyse their personal characteristics and their history with the trauma or other past traumas. Then, they evaluate the type of treatment to be chosen. These are a few of the treatments that are commonly used:

Cognitive-behavioral therapy: It helps you recognise your negative thoughts or unhelpful behavioural patterns and assists you in changing the way you think and behave.

Humanistic therapy focuses on self-liberation from self-defeating beliefs and attitudes. It is a therapy that focuses on the human potential and self-discovery.

Interpersonal therapy: a time-limited attachment-focused therapy for the resolution of interpersonal issues

Mindfulness-based cognitive therapy is an approach that combines cognitive therapy, meditation, and mindfulness.

4) PSYCHIATRISTS Psychiatrists are licenced mental health professionals who can prescribe drugs and medication. Typically, they favour a medication-first approach. They prescribe the dosage, potency, and duration of your medication based on its severity. However, once you begin taking your medication, you cannot abruptly discontinue treatment. These medications must be tapered off gradually, or your condition may recur.

Therefore, it is typically more beneficial when psychologists and psychiatrists collaborate. While the medication helps you immediately and cushions your recovery, the therapies treat the underlying cause, allowing you to heal rather than merely masking the symptoms. But regardless of which option you choose, know that no one but yourself can pull you out of this hole. They will all assist, motivate, and provide the necessary support, but you must do the actual work.

www.ingramcontent.com/pod-product-compliance
Lightning Source LLC
Chambersburg PA
CBHW050252120526
44590CB00016B/2318